She Came to Me a *Stranger*

GORDON BOSTIC

Primix Publishing
East Brunswick Office Evolution
1 Tower Center Boulevard, Ste 1510
East Brunswick, NJ 08816
www.primixpublishing.com
Phone: 1-800-538-5788

Published by Primix Publishing: 10/18/2024

ISBN: 979-8-88703-406-5(sc)
ISBN: 979-8-88703-407-2(e)

Library of Congress Control Number: 2024917428

Dedication

To my brothers, Jon and Tim, who have always been there for me.

She Came to Me a Stranger

She came to me a stranger
Although she seemed to know
Secret things about myself
That no one else should know.

She came to me a stranger
I've never met before
But with a certain aura
That I could not ignore.

She came to me a stranger
Whom I did not know well.
A passerby in journey
To where, she would not tell.

She came to me a stranger
And left me much the same.
We shared a brief interlude
But did not catch her name.

She Proved to Be the Spider

She proved to be the spider
And I . . . I was the fly.
She's the one who spun the web
And I just happened by.

She lured me with her favors
And made me to believe
She's the prize I need to claim
As love we can achieve.

Then once I was entangled
She moved in for the kill.
She proved to be the spider
And I was her next meal.

A Candle in My Window

There's a candle in my window
That burns only for you.
Which, hopefully, will guide your steps,
Your journey to see through.

There's a candle in my window
That burns throughout the night
As a beacon for your return
And as your guiding light.

There's a candle in my window
I placed there just for you.
To be a constant reminder
I sit and wait for you.

There's a candle in my window
So you can clearly see
That when your journey is complete
It'll guide you back to me.

My Epithet

Don't cry for me in my demise
It is my time to die.
I lived the life I wished to live
So there's no tears to cry.

I never did an evil thing
But lapses I have had.
I tried to do what I thought best
That have sometimes turned bad.

I leave this life with few regrets
Of errors I have made.
That's not to say there weren't mistakes
But most someone forgave.

I mostly did what I had wished
And touched a life or two.
Though none will claim that I was great
I paid what I thought due.

And in my passing I would like
My epithet to say:
"He merely was a mortal man
Who strove to find his way."

The Markers by the Road

We do not handle tragedy
The way we thought we would
As we race to build monuments
More quickly than we should.

We dedicate the tragic place
As symbol to our loss
And sanctify the tragedy
With trinkets or a cross.

We seem to think memorials
Will somehow set things right
So we set up tiers of candles
To gleam and glow at night.

We set up markers by the road
To note the tragedy
Ensuring that the passersby
Will have no choice but see

That in this spot somebody died,
And died most tragically.
That person was a friend of theirs
Or, maybe, family.

First You Must Believe

No matter what the effort is,
In order to achieve
The greatest of ingredients
Is first you must believe.

There are no great accomplishments
Nor praise can we receive
If we can't find the starting point
That first you must believe.

No wish has ever come to light
Nor dream can we conceive
If we don't recognize the fact
That first you must believe.

The Hanging Tree

It was a place we did not go
For memories recalled
Of all the sadness it had brought
To those that it had called.

Its gnarled branches that bore no leaves
For lo, these many years.
As it had not been fertilized
By the heartbroken tears.

It was a place where men were brought,
Unwilling and in chains.
Where on more than one occasion
They never left again.

It was a tree that bore no fruit
But evil and desire.
Many had sworn to cut it down
But it would fuel no fire.

All knew it as the hanging tree
Where justice was denied.
Whose trunk is haunted by the sounds
Of all of those who cried.

What's the Purpose of the Game?

They say that we should not keep score.
So why then play the game?
Why should we make the effort if
The ending is the same?

They say that winning is a sin
Because the losers cry.
So what's the purpose of the game
And where's the need to try?

For losing is an element
They wish hard to reject.
So no one has their feelings hurt,
We play to no effect.

Life's consumed in competition
That sport prepares us for.
So what's the purpose of the game
If we cannot keep score?

Come Lie with Me

Come lie with me beside the sea
Where passions can be freed.
Where expectations can be met
Filling the other's need.

Come lie with me upon the sand
Beneath a starry sky.
Where we can share all we may wish
And never caring why.

Come lie with me for just a while
Until there is no need
To share in close proximity
Our hunger yet to feed.

Come lie with me beside the sea
For comfort and console,
Where we can choose immerse ourselves
Within each other's soul.

The Dreams We Dare Not Dream

We all have dreams we dare not dream
For fear they may come true.
The dream I dream that I fear most
Is one involving you.

Sometimes they call them nightmares but
They're still dreams just the same.
Unconscious thoughts we won't reveal
For fear of where they came.

The dreams we wished we had not dreamed
For reasons we can't say.
That stay with us and linger on
And never go away.

They seem to speak of future times
With a dark clarity,
Of days we pray that will not come
Or simply will not be.

So we will try dismiss the dream,
Although the fears remain.
We've dreamed the dream we dare not dream
And suffer with the strain.

Our Burdens

Just yesterday, I saw a man
Who bore a heavy load.
In weariness he had collapsed
And lay beside the road.

So many people passed him by
Without a second glance.
In pity I had stopped to see
If I could help by chance.

I asked him if he needed help
And to that he said no.
He'd only need a moment's rest
And then he's good to go.

I asked if I could share the load
To which he merely sighed.
He studied me a minute more
Before he had replied.

He said his burdens were his own
From choices he engaged.
And how the load grew heavier
The more that he had aged.

Then as I stood and watched him go
It had occurred to me
The burdens that we all must bear
Are more than we can see.

I Want to Be a Part of You

I want to be a part of you
And have you part of me.
And know your kiss and warm embrace
As we lie by the sea.

I want to know the inner you,
The you, you really are.
And hold your form and dream with you
Under a drape of stars.

I want to share your dreams of love
Your life of years to come
And pledge to you my heart, my love,
Before the coming sun.

Success and Failure

We revel in accomplishments
We've worked hard to achieve.
And bask in all the accolades
We're grateful to receive.

We're humbled when we're given praise
We think is truly due
And shine in the acknowledgment
Of anything we do.

But failure we don't handle well
When it is pointed out.
We tend to become defensive
And willing to lash out.

We're happy in receiving praise
And angry when we don't.
We should accept the balances
But know we clearly won't.

The Thunder of the Drums

He heard the thunder of the drums
And instantly recalled
The horror that he once had faced
To which he had been called.

He feared the thunder of the drums,
That they may call again.
To whisk him off to foreign lands
Where he'd already been.

He loathed the thunder of the drums
And what the drums may mean.
The sights that he was sure to see
He had already seen.

He heard the thunder of the drums
And prayed they weren't for him.
For they had called him once before
And cost him soul and limb.

Lost to Our Technology

We're lost in our technology
So we don't understand
How to hold a conversation
Or touch another's hand.

We've become so isolated
Living within our phones
That we're lost to relationships
As something we've not known.

We reside in a cyber world
With answers on demand
But we've lost our ability
Our real lives to command.

We're strangers to reality
For we won't change our way
And step outside the cyber world
To see the light of day.

Mere Faces in the Crowd

The listless eyes and aimless walk
Of those who are not proud,
Who carry burdens we don't know.
Mere faces in the crowd.

Preoccupied with their own lives
To know that we exist.
They struggle with indignities
That surely we'd resist.

They live their lives oblivious
To those they do not know.
Uncaring of the weaknesses
Or scars they may not show.

Their burdens left for them to bear
In their anxiety.
As they ponder their existence
Within humanity.

They're merely faces in the crowd
We pass along the way.
And never give a second's thought
To what they have to say.

Who Was It That Decided

Who was it that decided
What colors were to mean?
That royalty is purple
And envy's marked as green.

That yellow means cowardice
And when we're sad we're blue.
That red is when we're angry
Or we could be hot too.

That black means that we're evil
And white means that we're good.
That blue is for baby boys
And pink means sisterhood.

Why does blue have more meanings
And orange has none at all?
That gray is indecision
Or questionable call.

Who was it that decided
What colors were to mean?
And why did we fall for that
Are reasons now unseen.

You Were Worth Fighting For

I've always done what I thought best
For better or for poor.
And in the end I'd hoped to find
You were worth fighting for.

For I withstood all your demands
To outlast all your beaus
And hoped to win over your heart
As I had loved you so.

It was the battle of my life
I fought so hard to win.
Not knowing what results may be
But trusting in the end

Now through the years we've had the chance
Together to explore,
That now I know with certainty
You were worth fighting for.

The Monster in the Lake

Ev'ryone had grown to fear
The monster in the lake.
No one had ever seen it,
But there was no mistake.

Prints were sighted on the shore
As proof that it was there.
But no one ever saw it
Or were willing to share.

Then one day a group of boys
Set out upon the lake.
To prove there was a monster
Or prove it was a fake.

As the hours slipped away
There still had been no sign.
So they began to believe
It was a waste of time.

Then something stirred beneath them
Which harshly rocked their boat.
Luckily they weren't capsized
As they remained afloat.

But they paddled hard and fast
Desperate to reach shore.
Gone was investigation
And needing to explore.

Whatever they encountered
Was not by some mistake.
Damage to the boat had proved
That something's in the lake.

They lived to tell their children
What had been a mistake.
The day they went searching for
The monster in the lake.

Nothing You Can Offer Me

There's nothing you can offer me
To prove that you've been true.
I've caught you in so many lies
I can't believe in you.

I don't know if you're capable
Of any honesty.
I know I'm not comfortable
With anything I see.

I cannot spend my life with you
In fear you won't betray
The hope and trust I placed in you
Won't just be thrown away.

So if in you I cannot trust
I'll have to walk away.
For I refuse to live my life
Not trusting what you say.

How Can I Know If I'm in Love?

How can I know if I'm in love
When I've not loved before?
I have the signs the poets sing
But surely there is more.

How can I know if what I feel
Means love has come my way?
The feelings seem so real to me
But they could go away.

How can I know if my heart beats
With passion and desire,
If they are both strangers to me
In what they may require?

How can I know if I'm in love
When I've not loved before?
For love is but a mystery
That I've yet to explore.

The Price of Freedom

The price of freedom has been high
As it has always been.
It's taken from us family
As well as other kin.

For freedom's a prize we value
So much we will not lose.
Regardless of the sacrifice
Or cost of freedom's dues.

Some say the price is way too high
For what we have received.
The right to live unencumbered
And do what we've believed.

So we pay the price of freedom.
Whatever that entails,
To ensure for our progeny
Our freedom never fails.

Imagine What the World Could Be

Imagine what the world could be
If we'd do as we should,
By treating others as ourselves
Or as we hope they would.

If when we make our promises,
We'd always follow through;
And ev'rytime we gave our word
That to our word we're true.

If we would be considerate,
Concerned with others' need.
Instead of hoarding for ourselves
In focus of our greed.

Imagine what the world could be
If effort we applied
In doing what we know to do
And on goodness relied.

You Were the One

You were the one who challenged me
To reach beyond the stars.
To not succumb to obstacles
But grasp for higher bars.

You were the one directing me,
Potential to apply.
You told me to face challenges
And always seek the why.

You were the one protecting me
From mistakes I would've made
And minimized the damages
When your faith I betrayed.

You were the one to comfort me,
Allaying all my fear.
You were the one I trusted most.
The teacher I held dear.

You were the one who stood by me
When no one else would stand.
You were the one to question me
So you could understand.

You were the one who urged me on
When I had hit a wall.
You were the one to pick me up
When I'd stumble and fall.

You were the one who guided me
When you had thought you should.
You were the one who trusted me
When I thought no one would.

You taught me to have confidence
In who I may become.
To ignore the criticism
That always seems to come.

You were the one who spoke for me
When words I could not find.
You're the one I relied upon
To grant me peace of mind.

Fog on the Mountain

It happened in the dead of night
When on a midnight run
A sense of doom had come to him
But reasons he had none.

The mountain was immersed in fog
So dense he could not see
The eighteen-wheeler bearing down
In his proximity.

The headlights were eclipsed by fog
So neither of them knew.
Their course had been the very same
And neither had a clue.

The impact made was at full bore
But neither knew a thing.
Their deaths were instantaneous
As that's what head-ons bring.

Now legend has it when the fog
Engulfs the mountainside,
Two eighteen-wheelers reappear
As to resume their ride.

Yet though they knew the other's there
The ending is the same
And the fog on the mountaintop
Is always held to blame.

A Penny for a Dream

Young Peter found a penny
And proudly showed his dad.
But Dad had been unimpressed
To see what Peter had.

"You only found a penny.
There's nothing you can buy."
Then his father stopped himself
For fear he'd make him cry.

But Pete stared up at his dad
With a face all agleam,
"If we can find a wishing well
It may well buy a dream."

It's Not Exactly Death We Fear

It's not exactly death we fear
But that we'll disappear.
Lost among the every day
As if we were not here.

To pass away without regard
For anything we've done.
Or fading into the ashes
Without a battle won.

Our fear is in the great unknown
Of what we leave behind
Such as not to be remembered
In anybody's mind.

It's not exactly death we fear
But that we've come and gone.
While the world revolves without us
As life simply moves on.

Footprints in the Sand

No matter who we think we are
Nor what our lives demand.
We leave behind a legacy
Of footprints in the sand.

At first our steps are very small
Until we take in hand
The measure growth will bring to us
Through footprints in the sand.

Ev'ry man must walk his own path
As he must understand
Life's a journey that's recorded
By footprints in the sand.

From mistakes we cannot walk back
To sorrows we withstand,
All milestones in our journey kept
As footprints in the sand.

Then when our journey's near its end
And we have lost command,
We can return to trace our steps
Through footprints in the sand.

There Are Those

There are those who set the course
And those who tag along.
There are those who merely dream
And those that don't belong.

There are those who change the map
That others will not draw.
There are those who dare to do
And those who stand in awe.

There are those who bravely stand
And those who run away.
There are those with promises
Who won't do what they say.

There are those who make a choice
And those easily swayed.
There are those who make themselves
And those who're ready-made.

There are those who'll change the world
And those who'll simply stare.
There are those with open hearts
And those who do not care.

There are those you can depend
To come in time of need.
And there are those you can't trust
Nor their advice can heed.

There are those who keep the faith
And those who don't believe.
There are those whom greatness picks
And those who won't achieve.

There are those who'll kill themselves
And those who'll simply die.
But all will stop to question,
Just how hard did they try.

I Saw a Man

I saw a man who's bleeding,
Just lying in the street.
People had stepped over him
So not to soil their feet.

I saw a man who's weeping
Just sitting all alone.
People quickly passed him by
While staring at their phone.

I saw a man reacting
To bad news he'd received.
People just avoided him
As if he were diseased.

I saw a man who's dying
And gasping for some air.
But people were blind to him
As if they did not care.

What truly has come of us
And our society
To strip us of our courage
And our humanity.

The Perfect Life

John Lee was a perfectionist
Which no one had denied.
He seemed to live a perfect life
Until the day he died.

They found his body hanging from
His valued chandelier.
And from the note he left behind
All nearly moved to tear.

But he'd not lived a perfect life.
He was a lonely man.
And found no reason to live on
The way he always had.

For what we think a perfect life,
Rarely turns out to be.
As lives are lived behind closed doors
In veils of secrecy.

How Hard You Hit Back

Don't moan and groan and whine to me
That you're under attack.
It's not about how hard you're hit
But how hard you hit back.

You choose to be a punching bag
Who never punches back.
Or you can stand up for yourself
And weather the attack.

No victory was ever claimed
By one who dared back down.
And no one ever comes to aid
Someone they think a clown.

In life two choices can be made:
To give up or attack.
It's not about how hard you're hit
But how hard you hit back.

Entitlements

Entitlements give credence to
The ones who won't achieve.
They live upon the benefits
That most do not receive.

They are robbed of their incentive
To take care of themselves
And strip from them their dignity
As boxes lined on shelves.

Entitlements have given us
A new nonworking class.
Who have no need to get a job
So sit home on their ass.

Entitlements aren't meant to help
But governmental ploy.
To build a righteous voting block
Of those they would destroy.

I Do Not Walk the Beaten Path

I am a lemming who won't leap
When all the others do.
A creature who pursues the night
As very few would do.

I am a member of the herd
Who fights to find his way.
Who won't pursue what others seek
But yearns to break away.

I am a hostage of the crowd
Who struggles to be free.
Who won't adopt what others think,
Only what I believe.

I will not be a legacy
To all that may be wrong.
I've never walked the beaten path
Because I don't belong.

Legislation Is a Game

We're close to having government
That's gone to pay-per-view.
Where legislation is a game
And no one gets their due.

Where their debates are televised
And all put on a show.
They argue about trivia
So people will not know

The issues that are of import
Is where they will not go.
Not one of them will take a stand
For fear what voters know.

So they perform upon their stage
And put on quite the show.
Where legislation is a game
Because it's all they know.

The Coward Dies a Thousand Deaths

He came to hear the drums of war
And knew they beat for him.
For all young men were called upon
Whenever times grew grim.

He answered to the drumbeat's call
As all the young men did.
Except for Andrew Butterman
Who ran away and hid.

They trained them for a little while
Before they dared to arm.
They said that only victory
Would keep them safe from harm.

So off they marched to the front lines
To jump into the fray.
Where they saw the scenes of conflict
And death, day after day.

They suffered losses over time
Until the war was won.
When their leaders praised their efforts
And told them they were done.

What had remained set out for home
To reclaim their lost lives
But as they drew closer to home
None could avert their eyes.

A body had been left for them
That hung down from a tree.
Around the corpse there hung a sign
For ev'ryone to see.

The body once was Butterman
The sign had hung upon.
"The coward dies a thousand deaths.
The brave man only one."

The Only One I've Known

You were the one to beckon me
When I'd no place to go.
The one who dared to shelter me
As one you did not know.

You opened up your heart and home,
Willing to take a chance
That something good would come of it
If just by happenstance.

You gave to me purpose again,
When I had none at all.
And showed me love I had not known
That helped me to stand tall.

You provided the direction
I found that I had need.
And supplied me with the comfort
To prove that you believed.

You're the one who chose to raise me
Which no one else would do.
Providing me with confidence
And strength to see life through.

You're the one who dared adopt me
And treat me as your own.
You gave to me a family—
The only one I've known.

A Glass of Water

Life is like a drinking glass;
Half empty or half full.
And ev'rytime we sip from it
A moment do we pull.

But it is not a simple glass
We can one day refill.
For once we take a sip from it
There's one less sip to spill.

Then slowly as the volume wanes,
Until there is no more.
We stare into an empty glass
Outside of heaven's door.

Don't Tell Me What I Ought to Think

Don't tell me what I ought to think.
My mind is mine alone.
I have the capability
To form thoughts of my own.

I'm not a parrot who repeats
What others have to say.
I make decisions on my own
And think in my own way.

Don't tell me what I ought to know.
Discovery's the key.
The thoughts that I am meant to think
Make me uniquely me.

Haunted by Appearances

They considered him a monster
Because he was deformed.
The product of a troubled birth
They were forced to perform.

Because of his deformities
He lived a lonely life.
He was rarely seen in public
As it caused so much strife.

Because people would avoid him
Or simply stop and stare.
They would speak of his appearance
As if he were not there.

And never had he known a friend
As people seemed afraid
To engage in conversation
With one who's ugly made.

So none knew of his capacity
For caring and for love.
All haunted by appearances
To see what he's made of.

The Jersey Devil

He saw it skulking through the woods
But thought it was not real.
It was demonic in its gait
And evil in its feel.

He stopped to watch it from afar,
Too afraid to approach.
And marveled at the stealthiness
In which it would encroach.

Then, suddenly, it turned and stared
As though it knew he's there
With eyes that were ablaze in red
And held an icy stare.

He was afraid to even breathe
For fear that it would know
That there was someone watching it
And cover he would blow.

He'd heard the stories as a child
But never had believed.
The Jersey Devil was for real
And it was looking peeved.

One moment it was standing there.
The next it disappeared.
So then he ran with all his might
Before it reappeared.

The Story of the Journey

The story's in the journey
Not where the journey ends
And it starts in the beginning
As the journey begins.

It's not the distance or the length
The story's apt to tell
But the nature of the journey
And if you journeyed well.

For all of life is a journey
That we must undertake
And the story of our journey
Is what's left in our wake.

Someone Walks with Me

I find that someone walks with me.
Someone that I should know.
Someone unseen who pushes me
So I may thrive and grow

I feel that someone walks with me
And guides me on my way.
A presence that I simply feel
That's with me ev'ry day.

I know that someone walks with me
My heart has told me so.
A guiding presence watching me
As through life I must go.

I fear that someone walks with me
Who knows better than me
The path that I should firmly walk
With truth and honesty.

She Came to Me a Stranger

She came to me a flashback
That I remember still
When we shared a span of time
And reveled in the thrill.

She came to me a vision
From deep inside the night
With promises of passion
Before the morning light.

She came to me an outcast
With nowhere else to go.
Shrouded in the mystery
That I would never know.

She came to me a stranger
As one I used to know
But once I learned to love her
She said she had to go.

The Margo Fair

They found their ship was sinking fast
With all hands still onboard.
There was no hope of saving it
As in the water poured.

There were no lifeboats to be had
For they'd been swept away.
There had been nothing they could do
But wait their fate and pray.

The *Margo Fair* went down that night
With all hands still on board.
They sank into the pitch-black sea
Where they would meet their lord.

But sometimes in the dead of night
Some say they've seen it rise.
Eerily lit, beneath the moon,
To glow against the sky.

It searches for its former course
As though it's not yet done.
It has a mission to complete
On this its final run.

The Ruins

I rummage through the ruins of
What once was a great race.
The vestiges that still remain
Are tributes to their trace.

Their architecture proves to me
How much they had to know.
And with that knowledge lost to time
How little's left to show.

I wonder how a populace
Completely disappears?
Leaving what they knew behind, to
Be lost for all these years.

The ruins are a testament
That people once lived here,
But saddened in the knowledge that
They could not persevere.

Unnoticed and Unknown

I don't deserve my lot in life
But that's the hand I'm dealt.
It's not as though I've not achieved,
But rather what I've felt.

I watch the undeserving ones
As they play with their toys.
While forced in struggle to survive,
Devoid of many joys.

I live beneath the wings of fame
Unnoticed and unknown.
I toil in anonymity
Regretting chances blown.

For once promise washed over me
As "golden boy" proclaimed.
A certainty to make it big
And fortune I would claim.

But I grew lazy in pursuit
Of goals that I had set
And saw my star begin to fade
As deadlines were not met.

So now I suffer with regrets
In living with my shame,
Knowing I could have had it all
With only me to blame.

Free Will

God, in his grace, gave us free will
To choose or not to choose
But we refuse to make a choice
For fear of what we'd lose.

As we live with indecision
And second-guess our dreams.
Afraid that in the choice we made
Is never what it seems.

So we stew on the consequence
Of what each choice may bring
And find that we are paralyzed
From doing anything.

Behind My Closet Door

Before I go to sleep at night
There's dread I must explore.
For something stirs when lights go out
Behind my closet door.

I know I've checked a thousand times
But nothing's there to see.
Though as soon as the lights go out
Up pops the mystery.

I've never ever heard it in
The middle of the day.
It only seems to rise and stir
When the light goes away.

I've tempered fear of hearing it.
I've heard it for so long.
It sometimes seems quite comforting
As if it may belong.

There's something that has shaken me
That I try to ignore.
For something stirs when lights go down
Behind my closet door.

Unlike a Normal Day

I see the vultures gathering
In search of naked prey;
And wonder if it's come to this,
The ending of my day.

As I reflect on what I've done,
There's sadness and regret.
But certain things I take great pride
In knowing challenge met.

I know my name will not be scrawled
On page of history.
And songs and stories not composed
For what I did achieve.

But hopefully, I've touched a life
In some small, special way;
And in my passing I'll be missed
Unlike a normal day.

Nothing in Life Is Free

There's nothing in this life that's free
As someone has to pay.
Our country is not rich enough
To just give things away.

For ev'rything in life has cost
And value that we prize.
If something then was to be free
The cost's kept in disguise.

For money is not limitless
It's finite by decree
And anything we give away
Is never truly free.

There's nothing in this life that's free
No matter what they say.
For ev'rything they say is free
Is paid for in some way.

The Offspring of the War

They were the offspring of the war.
The ones who had survived.
Those who believed the only tears
Were those that they had cried.

They were the victims of the war
Who lived with fear and dread.
The ones whose parents had been slain
And grew up with the dead.

They all were wounded in the war
With scars invisible.
No mercy ever shown to them
That was discernible.

They were the product of the war
For peace they never knew
A generation born to war
As that is all they knew.

Come Sail with Me

Come sail with me across the sea
To new lands to explore.
Where we may be the entity
Who first steps on that shore.

Come challenge me to test the sea
To see how far it goes.
And guess with me the purity
Of what it truly knows.

Come run with me beside the sea
For secrets it may hide.
Then answer me the mystery
That comes in with the tide.

Come stand with me within the sea
And feel the ebb and flow.
Then wait with me, reverently,
Until it's time to go.

All the Thoughts That Rush at Me

I hate it when I need to write
But words I cannot find
To tell the feelings that I feel
Or what is on my mind.

It's like the words are teasing me
Just outside of my grasp.
And though I try to reach for them
I find they're none to clasp.

I look upon the images
Of words I used to know.
But none of them will come to me
Although I wish it so.

So I stare at the empty page
With words I cannot find
As all the thoughts that rush at me
Are trapped inside my mind.

She Is

She is the wellspring of my soul.
The air I wish to breathe.
The promise I do not deserve
And barely can conceive.

She is the candle in the night
That serves to light my way.
She is the dream I dared to dream.
The prayer I would pray.

She is the joy I came to find.
The peace I've come to know.
The fount of passion that I've found
That drives my heartbeat so.

She is the one I cannot lose
Nor ever give away.
She is the one I value most
In each and ev'ry way.

She is the first thing that I view
When first I lift my head.
And she's the last thing that I watch
Before I go to bed.

Our Mistakes

Mistakes are but the stepping stones
From which wisdom is gained.
It's from mistakes we come to learn
And questions are explained.

Mistakes are but the building blocks
From which knowledge is grown.
It's placed into a reservoir
Of all we've ever known.

Our mistakes are fundamental
To who we may become
By overcoming our mistakes
To find where we came from.

Tryouts

Do not give me your excuses
For what you cannot do.
I demand to see the effort
That proves you will fight through.

Don't try to razzle-dazzle me
For I have seen it all.
I'm looking for ability
Both on and off the ball.

I look for personality
That fits into the team.
One willing to face challenges
And not afraid to dream.

But I will have no superstars
Or those that think they are.
For we will be one entity
That egos will not mar.

So show me ev'rything you've got.
Keep nothing in reserve.
I only take the very best
Who show the skill and nerve.

The Gift

It was a gift I did not ask
But came to understand
Some gifts we've not been looking for
Have turned out to be grand.

It was the gift I did not seek
But could not turn away.
For unexpected gifts are sweet
When they should come our way.

It was a gift I never thought
That I was ever due.
It was the best gift I've received
Because the gift was you.

I Never Let You Go

Now that my time is drawing nigh
There's something you should know.
The love we chose to abandon,
I never let it go.

Although it was so long ago
I clearly still recall
How happy we had been back then
Thinking we had it all.

But then you had a change of heart
Without a place for me.
So we went our separate ways
To start a new journey.

And ev'rywhere I've ever gone
I've carried thoughts of you.
Although you had been done with me,
I was not over you.

Now that my journey's at its end
I wanted you to know,
I always kept you in my heart
And never let you go.

Wanting to Belong

He had wanted to be normal,
As least, treated that way.
They said that he had special needs
Above the common fray.

He saw the way they looked at him,
With pity and remorse.
As though he was so different
They'd sometimes change their course.

He never thought differences
Should be how he's defined.
He knew he was a man apart
Who had been unrefined.

But in his heart he was the same
As any in the throng.
He did not care about his needs
But wanted to belong.

The Doubts Had Lingered

He knew he tried the best he could
But was it good enough?
He stared into her deep blue eyes
But feared that she would bluff.

No single word had either spoke
When rising from the bed.
So the doubt kept on lingering
And running through his head.

She bent to kiss him fore she left
And wished him a good day.
Whatever else was on her mind
She did not care to say.

Until that night when he came home
To a dark, lonely room.
He had not heard a word from her
Which left a sense of doom.

He thought he may enjoin a bar
Where he could sit awhile.
When came a knocking at his door
He opened to her smile.

The Truth

People see what they want to see
And never see much more.
They tend to see selectively
The rest they just ignore.

It's dangerous to see too much.
So they refuse to see.
The truth to them is obvious
And what it needs to be.

That's why the truth is never clear.
It's seen selectively.
For people only know the truth
That they decide to see.

A Light That Burns for Me

There is a light that burns for me
In hope that I come home.
To give up all my wandering
And my desire to roam.

There is a light that burns for me
That beckons through the night.
To guide me with its radiance
To comfort and delight.

There is a light that burns for me
I know will never fade.
As it summons with conviction
To light the path I've made.

There is a light that burns for me
That shines to call me home
When I'm done with wandering
And my desire to roam.

The Choices Made

Eventually we realize
It's our child's choice to make.
And whether we agree or not
We back them for their sake.

Not ev'ry choice that they will make
Is for us to approve.
We only hope the choices made
Will allow them to prove

That we have done our best by them
In guidance and command.
So they will know the choices made
Are ones they understand.

The Wasteland of Broken Dreams

I wander through the wasteland
Of all my broken dreams
And wonder what could have been
If I'd ignored the schemes.

I tried too many shortcuts
As I'd not understood
That dreams do not make themselves
And never ever could.

It takes a lot of effort
To make our dreams come true
But I had been unwilling
To give what I knew due.

So I wander the wasteland
Of all my broken dreams
And wonder what may have been
If effort were supreme.

We've Forgotten How to Laugh

We take ourselves so seriously
We don't know how to laugh.
Everything must be correct
And nothing is a gaffe.

There is no humor in the world
As we're so introspect.
That ev'ry little harmless joke
Is viewed as disrespect.

We think that we are more than we
Should ever grow to be.
As we're paragons of virtue
That no one else can see.

And from this we've derived a world
Where humor is not seen.
Where those that dare to tell a joke
Are ridiculed as mean.

A Better Man

Sometimes I wish I'd go to sleep
And wake a better man.
Someone who won't make the mistakes
That I most surely can.

A man who is wiser than me
In all so many ways.
Who won't waste opportunity
Nor while away his days.

Someone who knows what love can mean,
Not lost in one-night stands.
Someone who thrives on challenges
And won't sit on his hands.

Someone with purpose and desire
To be a bigger man.
Undaunted by the barriers
That he has yet to scan.

I wish that I could go to sleep
And wake to a new day.
Where I can be a better man
Than I have been today.

Some Choices

Some choices I am loathed to make.
Some choices are denied.
Some choices have been easy ones
And some left me surprised.

Some choices lead to great heartache.
Some choices let me down.
Some choices seemed just right for me
And some made me a clown.

Some choices I was forced to make.
Some choices I'd avoid.
Some choices were not winnable
And some were null and void.

Some choices were quite difficult.
Some choices left me blue.
But the one choice I don't regret
Is having chosen you.

We're Born with Possibilities

We're born with possibilities
That we may not achieve.
Sometimes because of laziness.
Sometimes we won't believe.

Sometimes because we're too afraid
To ever dare to dream.
Sometimes because we are unsure
We're truly what we seem.

Sometimes because we won't reach out
And try to touch a star.
Sometimes because of foolishness
That we won't go that far.

Sometimes because we're terrified
To see what we could be.
Sometimes because we're impotent
To act on what we see.

We're born with possibilities
More so than we would know
But we won't put forth the effort
To force ourselves to grow.

It Must Have Been the Moonlight

It must have been the moonlight
Reflecting from your hair.
That made me want to kiss you
And show you that I care.

It must have been the moonlight
That made your eyes gleam so.
That made me want to hold you
And never let you go.

It must have been the moonlight
That set your face aglow.
That made me want to touch you
And my affection show.

The only explanation
For how I've come to feel.
It must have been the moonlight
That made it all so real.

Everything I've Wished from Life

I marvel how the years have passed
And I still feel the heat.
For ev'ry time I look at you
My heart still skips a beat.

A lifetime spent in seeing you
'Most each and ev'ry day
Has not diminished how I feel
In any single way.

If anything, my love has grown
With passing of the years.
Knowing that you have seen my best
And also know my fears.

My love's given me foundation
Of all I think is true.
For ev'rything I've wished from life
I've found right here with you.

The Time Warp

I am trapped within a time warp
Of who I used to be.
And can't discard the images
Of who I thought was me.

The years have not been kind to me
As now I try to hide
The rebel that I used to be
Whose time I've tried to bide.

For once the things that I believed,
I still believe today.
It's just that I'm much wiser now
In what I choose to say.

But once, every now and then,
I hear the rebel yell
Awash in my indignation
I used to know so well.

And yet, I fear, those days are gone
As I'm too old to care.
I am caught within a time warp
Of now and then and there.

Why Don't Old Men Fight the Wars?

Why do we send young men to war
To fight the old men's fight?
If old men wish to have a war
Why don't the old men fight?

If war was such a noble thing
Why don't the old men go,
To fight for what they say is right
As only they can know?

The old men have much less to lose
Than those who are still young.
The ones who see life as a gift
From which they've barely sprung.

How many wars would there have been
If those who're in control,
Were forced upon the battlefield
And forced to pay the toll?

It's Through Our Failures That We Grow

It's through our failures that we grow
And learn to find our way
When mistakes become benefits,
Although sometimes we pay.

It's said that failure breeds success
Through knowledge that we gain.
The same applies to our own lives
In dealing with our pain.

For what once seemed catastrophic
May only shed some light
Onto a path or better way
That leads to some insight.

It's through our failures that we grow
As from mistakes we learn
We can find a new direction
From ev'ry twist and turn.

To Love a Bit Above

Although it's more than puppy love,
They were so very young.
They shared a bond that few could share
From which their love had sprung.

Their parents had objected to
How close they had become.
As both had thought they're way too young
For what they feared may come.

Their parents dared to interfere
And separate the pair.
But all that did was pull them close
In sharing their despair.

Thinking their parents had been wrong,
They planned to run away.
To find a place where they could love
With no one in their way.

But when the fateful night arrived,
In wait for her to come,
He held the tickets in his hand
When ev'rything went numb.

The bullet that had pierced his heart
Killed him before he cried.
And when, at last, she had arrived
She felt she too had died.

There was no reason to believe
The shot was meant for him.
A random shooting that was done
In times that had grown grim.

They found her inconsolable
As though death came for her.
But when they left her to her grief
It all became a blur.

No one was close enough to her
To stop her from her plan.
As all had watched in disbelief
The tracks to which she ran.

Together now forevermore
Eternally to love.
Two people who were very young
But loved a bit above.

The Ones the World's Not Worthy Of

Sometimes the world's not worthy of
The people it discards.
The people who live honestly
But find they have no cards.

The people who would strive each day
To try to pay their way.
The ones who live at the bequest
Of what others may say.

The people who may fight to live
Saddled in poverty.
The ones that wrap themselves in faith
Their lives aren't penalty.

The people who believe in truth
But live amid the lies.
The people who are quick to help
But find they've few allies.

Sometimes the world's not worthy of
Those who it would disdain.
Not part of high society
But the simple and plain.

The Friends That Drift Away

I've thought about them, once or twice,
The friends that drift away.
For once they meant the world to me
And then they'd slip away.

Most times it was not by their choice
As life has its demands.
But there were times the bond just fades
As if they're reprimands.

Sometimes I mourn for those I've lost,
And there're more than a few.
The friends that seem to drift away
With nothing I can do.

Life's Challenges

In life we must face challenges
Assured that some we'll lose.
But we are driven by the fact
We have the chance to choose.

Some challenges scare us to death.
Some we grow to adore.
Some challenges are difficult
And some we won't explore.

Some challenges we face head-on.
From some we run away.
But it is through the challenges
We fight to find our way.

For it's the measure of a man
With how he comes to grip
In handling the challenges
He faces in life's trip.

Truth Is Not That Obvious

How is it that you know the truth
When I am not that sure?
The answers all seem clear to you
While for me, they're obscure.

There seems to be some special light
Which allows you to see
The things that aren't so obvious
To someone such as me.

I never trust someone who thinks
Their answers are in tow.
For they can't see what's truly there
Is never what they know.

As ev'rything's not black and white
But many shades of gray.
And truth is not that obvious
No matter what they say.

The Alien

He said he was an alien
Who had just happened by.
His ship had suffered malfunctions
And would no longer fly.

So while the ship repaired itself,
He thought he'd look around
To find out if this world of ours
Was of any renown.

He saw pollution and the wars,
The poverty and pain.
The illnesses and the disease,
And lying just for gain.

He saw betrayal and the crime,
The murders and the theft.
He saw there was some good in us,
But not too much was left.

He hastily made his repairs
So soon he would be gone.
To find a better world that this,
The world he's standing on.

Who We're Meant to Be

We should not hide from who we are
Nor whom we're meant to be.
Although the person that we show
Is not who we may be.

We cloak ourselves in some disguise
To make sure they don't see
The person that we fear we are
Or that we're meant to be.

We live our lives pretending that
We're not who we may be.
In fear the person that we are
Is who we're meant to be.

We spend our lives in knowledge that
We have identity.
And though we try to hide from it
It's who we're meant to be.

Whatever We Can't See

Mankind has always been at odds
With what he cannot see
For if it can't be truly seen
How can it really be?

So man's suspicions start to grow
Of what he cannot see.
Not trusting in the probable
Of what may never be.

And then the fear comes into play
For trust man will not do.
If man can't put a name to it,
Man won't believe it's true.

So mankind is the last to trust
Whatever he can't see.
For if it is invisible
How can it really be?

Living the Dream

In truth he lived in poverty
But wished to make it seem
He was the icon of success
And was living the dream.

He lived a life of loneliness
But never would he deem
To submit to his solitude
As he's living the dream.

And when his health began to fail,
He never lost his beam.
Although his life was winding down
He's still living the dream.

Until the day his fight was lost
He hung on to the theme.
No burdens ever worried him
For he had lived the dream.

To Be Complete

Without the possibility
It all could end in pain.
There's nothing greater to be risked
For what there is to gain.

We spend our lives in endless search
Attempting to complete
That part of us we feel is lost
Or, somehow, incomplete.

Engaging in a wide array
Of temporary flings.
While praying that the one we've met
Will bring to us three things.

The passion that we so desire.
The comforting we need.
And in the end to be complete
The way that we believed.

Solitude

I've come to cherish solitude
As that is what I've known.
I have no need of company
Nor friendship to be shown.

My solitude has given me
A sense of inner peace.
I live where no one touches me
So tears I won't release.

I find that in my solitude
I do not have to feel.
Where I can never be exposed
To anything that's real.

I've found I've chosen solitude
As what I had to do.
So I'll not have to dwell upon
The pain of losing you.

The Rumor Mill

How many people have been harmed
From some revengeful lie;
Some fabrication that was spread
And they do not know why?

How many people have been hurt
From what's the rumor mill;
From innuendo and deceit
That rumors must instill?

How many people have been shamed
By gossip in the wind;
Half-truths that only seem to grow
And just as quickly bend?

How many people may have died
Responding to the tales
That have no purpose but defame
And dignity assails?

The Dance

They had danced the dance for years
But neither would admit
That feelings they fought to hide
Could be a part of it.

They would rumba to the tune
That neither chose to hear.
Denying the emotions
That both had grown to fear.

So for years they danced the dance
As neither would admit
The mystery they ignored
Was really part of it.

So it was they danced through life
As neither would admit
That ev'rything they had felt
Were at the heart of it.

A Corrupting Force

There was no way that he could see
He had another choice.
The people were in need of help
And he must be their voice.

He saw their burdens grow and grow
With no hope of relief.
The government had overreached,
At least, that's his belief.

Petitioning on their behalf,
He tried to plead their case.
But they had been oblivious
To what the people face.

They had a country they must rule
For which they had to pay.
The people were responsible
For paying their own way.

He told them that this can't go on.
He'd seen the people bleed.
They were the ones responsible
To meet the people's need.

The government was quite unmoved.
They had no need to care.
The people lived in poverty
While all of them lived there.

As history has clearly shown,
Disparity abounds.
For power's a corrupting force
Whose limits know no bounds.

Salvation When in Need

Whenever darkness was a threat
The people grew to pray.
But when the darkness was long gone
The people turned away.

Why is it we expect to find
Salvation when in need,
But we lose the motivation
Should the danger recede?

Valor on Display

Bravery had surrounded them
And courage stood them well.
But their leadership betrayed them
And now they're bound for hell.

The valley had been ringed with death
With cannon by the score.
They were told they would weather it
In honor of the corps.

Into the valley rode the corps.
Their valor on display.
Besieged by thunder of the guns,
Their numbers chipped away.

But on and on they bravely road
Until they were no more.
The valley that had claimed the lives
Of all within the corps.

Now legend only speaks of them
As valor on display.
The corps betrayed by leadership
Completely wiped away.

She Came to Me a Stranger

She came to me a stranger
But left me as a friend.
In between we formed a bond
I pray will never end.

She came to me a novice;
Unproven and untried
But left with a confidence
That I have been denied.

She came to me a tutor
With what I wished to learn,
And went about her lessons
With tender, kind concern.

She came to me a partner
Whose company I shared.
Coupled in the dark of night
When no one else had cared.

About the Author

Gordon Bostic was born in West Virginia and grew up in Virginia. A graduate of James Madison University and Fairleigh Dickinson University, he worked as a computer scientist and a software engineer for most of his life. He began writing at a young age as a way of expressing himself, his feelings, and his view of the world. Gordon has also had an interest in telling his stories in one way or another. *She Came to Me a Stranger* is his third novel. Gordon currently lives on the Jersey Shore with his wife, Susan.

www.ingramcontent.com/pod-product-compliance
Lightning Source LLC
Chambersburg PA
CBHW021113130726

47988CB00003B/1011